Praise

Winner - 2015 Goodreads Choice Awards — Poetry (*The Dogs I Have Kissed*)

"Gut truths and gin-clear imagery, Trista Mateer reminds us of all those places left unexplored by language."
— *Foreword Reviews*

"This is a collection that will beg you to be dog-eared, coffee-stained, and shared."
— Amanda Lovelace, Author of *The Princess Saves Herself in This One*

"With *Honeybee*, Trista has captured in amber something beautiful and tragic, joyful and painful."
Iain S. Thomas, Author of *I Wrote This For You*

"Bitter sweet with memory and softness, this book is an intimate and profound look at sexuality, heartbreak, loneliness, loss, love, healing and everything in between."
— Nikita Gill, Author of *Your Soul Is A River*

"How can something that hurts so much still be so tender? Mateer triumphs in this exploration. We are humbled to be witness."
— Ari Eastman, Author of *Bloodline*

"In *Honeybee*, Trista Mateer pulls the layers back on an old love and invites her readers to pick apart the pieces with her. She spares no one and nothing and the result is beautiful and awful and gorgeous and gut-wrenching."
— Fortesa Latifi, Author of *No Matter The Time*

"Trista writes about love so honestly. It's messy, reckless hope. It's sticky-fingered stubbornness. This collection is a must-read for any queer femme, and for anyone who has ever lost themselves in a feverish want."
— Clementine von Radics, Author of *Mouthful of Forevers*

honeybee

POEMS BY
TRISTA MATEER

central
avenue
publishing

2018

Published by Central Avenue Publishing, an imprint of Central Avenue Marketing Ltd.
www.centralavenuepublishing.com

HONEYBEE

978-1-77168-136-0 (pbk)
978-1-77168-137-7 (epub)
978-1-77168-138-4 (mobi)

Published in Canada

Printed in United States of America

1. POETRY / LGBT   2. POETRY / Subject & Themes - Love

10 9 8 7 6 5 4 3

for her,
wherever she is
but for myself too

POET DEMANDS
THE FLOOR!

a note from the author:

Years ago, a girl I used to love drove across state lines to get to a poetry reading, pulled out a piece of notebook paper, and approached the feature. I don't know what she said, but she came home with a handwritten note addressed to me from my favorite poet that read: "Trista, keep writing! The world needs your voice! Loud Loud Loud!"

I took it under consideration but I didn't really start writing until she left. It was long, and it was drawn out, and you can thank Andrea Gibson for the fact that it was Loud.

Honeybee is a collection about letting go, and like anyone who's ever successfully let anything go will tell you, you have to feel everything before you can put it down. What this means is that letting go is rarely a straightforward process. It's messy and it's repetitive, and it happens in waves of trying to make things work and trying to move on at the same time. If I've done my job right, this book reflects that. I wrote it as things were unraveling. I put the original versions of these poems out into the world before things were truly over, because I wanted things to be over. This book, as it sits here now in its entirety, is an honest admission that something has ended.

I still write about it from time to time. I still press my fingers to the bruise. That's okay. So many people have reached out to me since I started sharing this work online. You all asked if it got better and I said, yes. Yes.

It's not the same hurt anymore.

In The End

I am going to hurt you.

You are going to hurt me.

But we will do it with practiced fingers
and passionate mouths
and I swear to God

it will be worth something.

Petrichor

Shoes muddy from all that kicked up dirt and last night's rain.
Faces flushed from walking. It is September,
still mostly summer-warm and
      you have your hand in mine.

In the parking lot of Hoffman's Home Made Ice Cream,
we're taking turns sucking up a chocolate shake and
      I can taste your chapstick
      left over on the straw
      every time I stick it in my mouth
      and pull.

We're nervous, laughing because this
is the closest thing to kissing we can do where people will see it.

      And you say, *it's always going to be like this, isn't it?*
                  All soft, and breathless.

      I say, *I hope not.*

Tenderness In Brevity:

her lipstick stuck to the side
of my best coffee cup, post-wash

Spun Sugar

The apples of your cheeks
taste more like strawberries:
sticky-sweet and pink. We're young
so everything sits on the tongue like this.

Everything is a promise
or a bottle of vodka mixed with lemonade.
A dress covered in sunflowers.
An overturned picnic basket.

Your blush, a cascade of color
from ballet shoes to fairy floss.
Your skin, like spun sugar.
It draws all the ants
to the spread we make of each other.

No longer just girls,
because love has turned us inside out.

You are the first thing in a long time
that has made me want to write
poetry again.

Hands In The Sun

Your touch
gets me so tender,
everything comes up
black and blue.

My heart
looks like a bruise
and I almost don't mind.

God, I almost don't mind.

IF I WERE A PEACH, YOU
WOULD BE THE PIT
THAT HOLDS ME ALL TOGETHER.

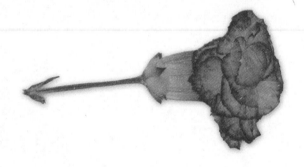

Our Own Vine And Fig Tree

When you go away to college, you don't ask for
your books back. I take your copy of *Everything Is
Illuminated* and highlight every passage about love.

I keep it in the soft place, with the walls made of
crushed red velvet, and I wait for you to find your
way back to the world we made for each other,

the place where it was safe for you to want me.

Going Through The Motions

Loneliness aims to make a spectacle of me
and I let it.

I stutter in polite conversation.
I forget how to say my own name.

I don't know what I am doing here without you.

You Tell Me Whenever You've Met A Boy Your Parents Will Like (Which Is To Say, Any Boy With A Working Knowledge Of Suburban White Christianity)

Conversations about him always start the same way. You say, *I want to marry a musician. I want to have five children. I want to be able to see my future unfolding out in front of me like an interstate map.*

I usually don't say anything at all.

I juggle the names behind every other tongue in your mouth: *Peter, Matthew, David, Adam.* Each one comes with the promise of things I don't know how to give you.

The Baker's Lament

You know the way you feel right before the kitchen timer goes off and you pull something fresh and full of cinnamon out of the oven? That moment made up of waiting. Nothing exists but you and the clock and the promise of something sweet and warm.

That's how I feel right before you walk into a room. When I can hear your footsteps on the floorboards but you haven't quite reached the door. And in that moment, everything is fine. Everything is more than fine. Everything is dusted-flour fingertips and your sister's laughter down the hall. Everything is sugar-coated.

I know this isn't going to end well, but I don't think it matters. I'm still stuck in that moment right before the timer goes off.

Everything is perfect. Everything is fine.

I slept incredibly well before I met you.

Questions For Small Town Girls
(Who Like Kissing Girls)

If her mother brings up Leviticus in polite conversation
and my mother laughs when she hears the word bisexual,
how much room do we have to breathe
in the middle?

Is it me that makes this wrong
or is it my body
or is it what I want to do with my body?

How do you effectively hold onto something
that you don't want other people to see in your hands?

What if I want other people to see it?

Perks

we grab coffee
every Tuesday at a shop
around the corner from my house
and when the cashier asks
if the order is together or separate,
she used to always say,
together

Untitled

I feel you on the edges of me
when you used to be in the center
and I don't know if this is worth
putting a name to.

You Break The News Like Bread At The Table

By which I mean, we are in Panera when you bring up The New Boy and his holy, holy mouth. The endless possibility of him. The miracle of his breath on your skin and every assurance behind it.

You tell me that he kisses like security, like a vow, like a big church wedding with your mother crying and your father stoic, but happy.

You tell me that this doesn't have to change anything between us.

Your phone goes off and you smile the same way you used to when I brought you flowers or wrote you poetry. Fruit punch is staining your mouth red and for the first time, I wonder about the cost of tasting it.

In Which Fear Sleeps Between Us

You call it a sin when we kiss
and you only hear the word unholy
in your mother's voice.

What a slow way to die, baby.
Day after day after day.

You Couldn't Just Leave?

You had to stand there saying:

*I love you, I love you, I love you
we're soul mates, you and I, but that doesn't mean it works
that doesn't mean it works*

that means my soul can't bear to be without yours

but that doesn't mean it works

Postscript

You said,
I know it always sounds like I'm saying goodbye, but I'm not.
And you were right.

I am the one saying goodbye.

I'M NOT SORRY. ~~I'M DOING THE RIGHT THING~~.
I SWEAR I'M DOING THE RIGHT THING. I HAVE
ABSOLUTELY NO DOUBTS ABOUT WALKING AWAY
FROM YOU. ~~THIS IS THE BEST THING~~. THIS IS
FOR THE BEST. I HAVE TO DO THIS. I AM BAD
FOR YOU AND SOMETIMES YOU ARE BAD FOR
ME AND THIS ISN'T WORKING ANYMORE.
NOTHING IS ~~XXXXXX~~ WORKING ANYMORE.
I DON'T KNOW HOW TO TALK TO YOU
WITHOUT FEELING LIKE NOTHING I HAVE
TO SAY IS IMPORTANT ENOUGH OR WISE
ENOUGH OR GOOD ENOUGH. I DON'T FEEL
GOOD ENOUGH ANYMORE. YOU DON'T MAKE
ME FEEL GOOD ANYMORE. I DON'T MAKE
YOU FEEL GOOD ANYMORE. ~~I HAVE TO DO~~
~~THIS~~. I HAVE TO DO THIS. PLEASE DON'T
PRETEND YOU DIDN'T FEEL THIS COMING
ON. WE'VE BEEN CIRCLING THE DRAIN FOR
MONTHS NOW. I'M SO SICK OF SPINNING.

WE BOTH HAVE THINGS TO DO AND WE TRIED
DOING THEM TOGETHER BUT IT JUST DOESN'T
WORK. WE JUST DON'T WORK ANYMORE.
~~I KNOW WE USED TO.~~ I SWEAR WE USED TO.
I FEEL SICK. I FEEL LIKE I TOOK TOO MANY
TURNS ON A CAROUSEL WITH A STOMACH
FULL OF SODA POP. I HAVE TO DO THIS.
I WANT THINGS THAT YOU DISAPPROVE OF
AND YOU WANT THINGS THAT I CANNOT GIVE
YOU. YOU STILL HAVE TIME TO DO EVERYTHING
YOU WANT TO. I PROMISE. YOU JUST HAVE TO
LET ME STEP OUT OF THE WAY. KEEP
COUNTING THE NAMES OF YOUR HYPOTHETICAL
CHILDREN BEFORE YOU FALL ASLEEP. KEEP
KISSING OTHER PEOPLE ~~SOMEBODY ELSE~~
GOODNIGHT. I HAVE TO DO THIS. I HAVE
TO. I HAVE TO GET THE FUCK OUT OF HERE.

I Fucked Up

I don't remember anything before you.
I never even understood the way light could flood a room
until I saw you walk into one.

Walking away from you feels like not taking care of myself.
It feels like sleeping too long and never eating breakfast
and forgetting to exfoliate.
It feels like nervous hands and paper cuts.

Restlessness.

Irritation.

A Wish

one day
we stop looking for our keys
and pick each other like stubborn locks
that won't open for anyone else

DO YOU REMEMBER
THE DAY I TOLD YOU
THAT YOU WERE MY
RHYTHM?

I AM ALL
SWAY AND STUMBLE.

MY FEET ARE COMPLETELY
LOST WITHOUT YOU.

Leftovers

In the produce section, I think I hear your name, but no one is around. I want to call you up right now and ask you to dinner.

I knew that I loved you when I started catching myself daydreaming about making grocery lists with you, rinsing romaine in your kitchen sink, knowing where your silverware drawer was without having to double check. I feel so lost today that all I want is to take your spare key from under the mat and make sure I still know where you keep your measuring cups.

I want to take a spill in aisle three just so I can run home to you and ask you to put your hands on me again. Like a bag of frozen peas, I want to press you up against everything sore.

Another Obligatory Poem Comparing A Girl To Something Consumable

She was the whiskey:
a hard hit with a slow burn.
I was the chaser.

The Ocean Always Looked Like You

I don't see her eyes and think of salt spray.
I see waves and think of her turbulence.
I see sand and think of the way
she has beat me to a pulp with her mouth.

She does not remind me of anything;
        everything reminds me of her.

The First Apology

I'm sorry for trying to love you
before I knew what I was doing.
The next person I kiss
is never going to touch the parts of me
that you held onto.

Honeybee

So I thought I could walk away from love and it would let me.
I thought distance might feel less like pulling on a rubber band
until it snaps back—but take a look at this: see all the red on me?

I've been staring at your letter for two days. Opened it at the
kitchen table, didn't even start crying until the third read-
through. It doesn't sound anything like you. Or it does and I just
don't want it to.

Does it make it better if I understand the anger, just not what
you buried it in? Does it make it better if I miss you even after
reading that?

I wrote you more poems than anyone else I ever kissed. I still held
your hand after you broke my heart. You told me that love meant
giving and giving and giving but at some point, all the plants
drown. You never told me that part. We outgrew each other in
angry, uncoordinated ways and I'm sorry for that.

If it helps, my chest still hurts when I think about your hands. If
it helps, I'm not sure I even know how to let you go.

You said: *most days I pity you more than I love you.*

I just love you.

Young Love As A Whetstone

Do you know what makes me more sad
than all of our mangled-up promises?

One day I will forget your soft, pink skin
and your wide smile. You will be

only

a thing that is hard to me,
something full of sharp edges.

I will not remember why I wrote all of these poems.

How I Asked You To Stay

I turned myself inside out over the phone,
read you the words etched on my bones and I
hoped for once they might settle your heart
instead of speeding it up.
And I know—I know I have a heart like a wild thing
with snapping jaws and matted fur
but I'd hang up my hands on hooks for you,
pluck out all of my sharp teeth
for the chance to be
easy.

How You Left

There was very little poetry involved.

Shedding

Giving my things back:
I am too heavy to carry
under the
weight
of all this new happiness.

I was as close as skin to you once.

Love was a museum where we took down the art that was there before us and played masterpiece with all the empty space.

Google Searches On The Verge
Of A Nervous Breakdown

cheap flights / sometimes I don't feel like a person / inability to
leave my bed / inability to breathe / things are moving very slow
but also very fast at the same time / symptoms of depression
/ how long do I have to sit in the sun before my brain starts
working right again / cheap flights / can you buy NyQuil in bulk
/ top ten foreign cities to disappear in / cheap flights / how to
explain anxiety to your mother / how to explain depression to
your mother / how to explain sometimes wanting to kiss girls
to your mother / what to do if you come out and your parents
don't love you anymore / how to find the city farthest away from
where you are currently at / cheap flights / how to pronounce
Melbourne / deadliest animals in Australia / will wanting to die
feel different in another country / does it matter

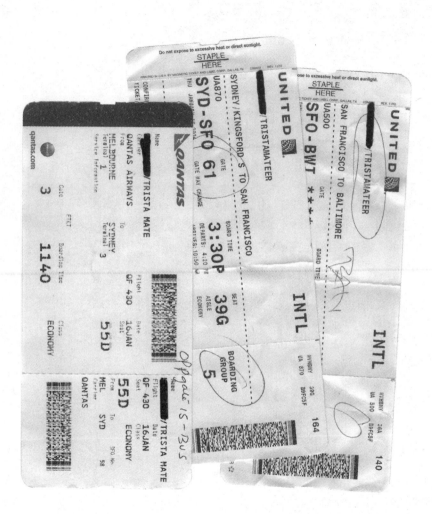

Phases

When I met you,
I was something
small and whole.
I do not know how
to get back there.

I Promised No More Poetry

I'd rather think of this
as a confession:

you are still the first person
I want to share new things with.

A List Of New Things

1. I had to ask for directions seven different times in LAX. It's a monstrosity built almost entirely out of anxiety. It's a shrine to nervousness.
2. I couldn't sleep for any of my twenty-four hour flight because I was worried I'd end up with my head on the stranger next to me or the flight attendant would want to ask me a question like, *who are you traveling with*? And I'd have to say no one. And I couldn't decide whether it was better to be awake and embarrassed or asleep and embarrassing. I kept doing that hypnagogic jerk thing over and over and I only know what it's called because you told me.
3. Yesterday I sat at a bar with a stranger and we practiced swallowing each other's accents.
4. Before I left, my mother said that she didn't care what I did in Australia, as long as I didn't get into the ocean because she's worried about great white sharks. Today I walked straight into the Pacific anyway. There are a thousand ways to get caught up in something's jaws.
5. Someone told me that despite the snakes and the spiders and the poisonous marine life, if we're judging by deaths caused per year, one of the deadliest creatures in this country is the European honey bee.
6. There's a constellation here called the Southern Cross that you can't see from the United States mainland. Every part of my life has pieces of you in it but this one.

Melbourne

I wish I could fall in love with this city
the way that I fell in love with you:
quick and over coffee.

Palm To Palm

I am not sorry it's over,
but I think my hands might always ache
for the symmetry of yours
and I hope you understand that now
as well as you used to.

Luna Park

I know we are both struggling with recognizing bad things and
letting them go but I need you to know:

I am the bad thing. (I was not always the bad thing. Sometimes it
was you. Sometimes it was just the two of us together.)

There were nights I was so jealous that the thought of you on
your knees for Jesus made me upset. Baby, I don't think you
understand the level of insecurity it takes for someone to want to
write God angry letters.

Do you remember the days you were so afraid to lose me that you
wouldn't say anything honest? You lived on eggshells, all pent up
anger and swallowed arguments. People can't function like that.

A few days ago, I was walking past this amusement park by
the beach. The front gate was the wide, smiling mouth of an
enormous sun.

I couldn't remember the last time I'd been happy.

Gum Trees

The first time I drove through
Australian bushland, I saw scorched
trees twisted up towards the sky.
Everything was black and brown
and gray and green. There are plants
there that need fire to germinate, to
crack their seeds, to grow, to change.
Heat thrust through the soil can stir
up things that were lost years ago.
Everything comes back after a bushfire.

I could start over after you.

For Everyone I Meet With Your Name

I'm sorry.

Avant La Haine

The best version of us is caught in a photograph where your arms exist permanently around me. Everything drips pink and gold in the sun as you laugh with your head back. I wear a dress covered in sunflowers and you hold me like a bouquet. Here, love gets to be hungry. Here, love never has its fill.

What I Wish Someone Had Told Me About Leaving (What I Can Tell You About Leaving)

i.   It is as hard to be the one who goes as it is to be the one who stays. People always talk about getting left behind, but nobody talks about how difficult it is to pack up your books and dig your bobby pins out of couch cushions. Every time you leave the house, it gets harder to walk back in. One day, you won't be able to.

ii. That is okay. It is okay to leave. It is okay to feel smothered by the weight of a life you didn't want or a relationship that doesn't taste the way you thought it would. It does not make you hard or disagreeable or unreasonable.

iii. Some people will leave. Some people are born flight risks. It is no shortcoming of yours that they cannot keep their feet on the ground. It is not your fault that they cannot seem to stand in place. They are not leaving you; they are just leaving. Realizing this does not make it better or worse.

iv. Some people will leave you. It will have everything to do with you and nothing to do with outside circumstances. You cannot sugarcoat it. You cannot dress it up and make it feel sweet or soft or warm. And it's going to hurt you. I know your instinct will be to beg them to stay, to unpack their bags for them, to curl up by their wandering feet—but people are going to leave you. That is okay too.

v.   Whether you are coming or going, leaving or staying, you're a moving part of something. We're all moving parts of something. Sometimes other people will sync up with us for a while, but you're still on the right path for you whether you're ticking along it alone or not. You are not defined by the people you walk away from, and you are not defined by the people who walk away from you.

This Has Nothing To Do With You

I feel like I've been sleepwalking for the last
three months. I am sick of the length of my hair
and the reasons I have to keep my nails short.
I keep forgetting how to breathe.
I keep forgetting how to be kind to myself.
I need to remember to berate myself with my
inside voice, to pick myself apart quietly
instead of making such a big fuss about breaking.

This Has A Little To Do With You

Today I bought sixteen mangoes.
I accidentally left the house without a bra on.
I forgot to wash my hair again.
I am having some trouble keeping it together.

I Have A Postcard Mouth

All it ever says is:
wish you were here.

What I Would Tell You If I Were Not Stubborn

You are not the moon or the sun, a planet or a dwarf star. I am not stuck in your gravitational pull. You are a girl too far away, with chapped lips and messy skin and yellow hair—and I love you. Maybe that is the same thing.

I am sorry—yes, because things ended—but also because I took your love for granted, treated it like a thing that you could never yank away from me. When you took the scissors I had pressed into your palms and cut our strings, I slipped out of step like a ruined marionette. I did not know how to cope with myself, did not know how to handle me-without-you.

I took three years of Spanish in school and still remember the basics. I've had twenty-two years to figure myself out, but after you, I need a crash course in my own body language. I don't remember what to do with my verbs when you are not around to conjugate them.

You were right when you said I've only had bad examples of love. I grew up thinking that it was a chore, that it did not have to be easy, that it was okay to be hard.

But ours was the exchange that defined "love" for me: unconditional even when it was distanced, never arrogant, always kind. And then one day there were conditions. I never planned on you being one of those bad examples.

After it was over, had been over for months, I told a friend that if you ever called, I would come running. And he said to me: *well, I guess it isn't over then.*

I know I said some things about needing space—but you are not the moon or the sun, a planet or a dwarf star. I do not know if distance from you will ever sit right with me (even if it has to).

(I think it has to.)

Daily Untruths

1. Things have gone too far.

2. There's no coming back from this for us.

3. My heart barely trembles
   when I shove it toward a stranger.

I KEEP THINKING
ONE DAY
I'LL WAKE UP
AND NOT LOVE YOU ANYMORE,

JUST LIKE THAT.

Wreck Of Loch Ard

I do not know if you were the coast and I was the sea,
or if we were the ship and the rocks were made of distance,
voices stretched thin, hearts that grew too hard
to say stop and too stubborn to give out.

All I know is that there were no lifeboats except for your arms,
and once, there existed depths that did not swallow us
but spit us up wet and willing to run right back in.

Semi-Factual Thoughts On Space

Did you know that when a star implodes,
for a few days, it can be brighter than an entire galaxy?
I still have light in my eyes from the way that you left me;
I still wait for my core to collapse like a black hole
and suck everything into it
when I meet someone else with your name.

Moons And Stars And Second-Guessing

Sorry I'm still writing about space when I think of you.
Truth is, I'm still trying to convince myself that we need it.

I called you *honeybee* for seven years. Now the bees are disappearing and so are you. I'm trying my best not to find this poetic.

On Every Body That Came After You

There is an emptiness here
that I swear was not there before
and I am doing my best
to fill it.

Forty-Four Sunsets

Last night, I curled up in the mouth of a man
who kept a copy of *The Little Prince*
on his nightstand.

I keep trying to lay myself down next to people
who understand the taste of loneliness
and don't mind it in their beds.

Most Days I Pity You More Than I Love You: A Short Study Of Bigotry And Hypocrisy

When a girl who used to leave her heart in my teeth
says I can't seek out happiness or truly know myself
as a person without first knowing the "real love" that only
a man can provide, I wonder how many days now sit
stagnant between the last time she called me her soul mate
and the first time she called me a slur. I want to ask her
about those nights we fell asleep inside each other, about
how much she must hate her own tongue. Her own hands.
The ticklish bends of her knees. All that skin I put my
mouth on. Amazing, all the things you can look past when
Christ gets involved. Amazing, all the things you can't.

My worth is not defined by a man and neither is yours.

So We're In Bed, Right?

And he leans over and says to me, *I've been reading your poems.*
You're proper heartbroken, aren't you?

First I curse at God, then at OKCupid, then at my own easily
Google-able name. Then at this man who has the audacity to
start talking about the state of my heart when I'm still naked in
his bed. Someone else's bed. With the wrong fingerprints all over
me and salt in my mouth. I twist out of his sheets to find my
clothes and he

asks what your name is.

A Brief Note On Biphobia

I'm not
  going through a phase
  using it as a stepping stone
  more likely to cheat on you
  just greedy
  secretly actually gay
  secretly actually straight
  inherently also polyamorous
  promiscuous because of my sexuality
  only into and always up for threesomes
  still trying to make up my mind
  attracted to all genders equally
  attracted to anything that moves
  experiencing less discrimination
  benefitting from "passing privilege"
  more likely to spread STDs
  heterosexual while I'm dating a man
  homosexual while I'm dating a woman
  transphobic
  or confused

but I am
  tired

Here's Your Permission

It is okay to spend your grocery money on wine and hair dye. Sometimes you have to.

Sometimes you have to drink shower beers and go out with strangers to places you never would have gone before — like an amateur comedy show in the basement of a hostel or a Monet exhibition at an art gallery. A silent disco. A poetry reading.

Go on vacation with someone else's family. See the way they treat each other. Remember how you would like to be treated.

Sometimes you need to run away from your problems even though you can't really outrun them. Move house. Change cities. Change countries. Take a trip. Breathe in air that has never witnessed your heartbreak before. And then let it out.

Keenan

People enter our lives in all sorts of inexplicable ways. They leave like that too but for once, I'm not focused on the leaving. I'm focused on the pack of fruit punch on your bedroom floor and the Chuck Klosterman books on your dresser. The comfortable warmth of your body next to mine. The night you said you didn't want to complicate things, so we shared our worst internet dating stories instead of kissing. The odds of me flying across the world to just end up meeting another American girl with the same name as my ex. The way I'm always gravitating towards home.

Bless My Bad Roommate

Bless the jacket I left on the plane.
Bless the parts of this heartbreak I left in an airport.
Bless the airport and their $14 salads
and the swelling in my ankles.
Bless the bank that botched my international transfer
and the two weeks I spent unable to feed myself.
Bless the fresh kiwi in someone else's fruit bowl.
Bless my bad roommate.
Bless her cold shoulder.
Bless the mattress on her bedroom floor
and the night she kicked me out.
Bless the house on Chaucer Street
and the girls who slept there.
Bless the chickens in the backyard.
Bless the fold out couch.
Bless the anxiety that got me up in the morning
even if it was just to make sure the door was locked.
Bless the whiteboard in the kitchen
and the hand on the dry erase marker
and the voice that said,
I know this isn't what you wanted it to be
but you can still make something good out of it.
Bless all the good I made out of it.

METROPOLITAN MUSEUM OF ART

FEDERATION SQUARE

OLD MELB GHOST TOUR

✳ THINGS TO DO

HOT JAM DONUTS!

JAM DONUT SHOPS!!

GO ON A DATE   GO ON A BETTER DATE

LORD OF THE FRIES ♡ ♥

WRITE A POETRY BOOK?

SEE BUSHLAND

LUNA PARK

ST KILDA   REAL AUSTRALIAN BEACH

FLINDERS STREET STATION

GOLDEN SYRUP DUMPLINGS

THE GREAT OCEAN ROAD

BALLARAT   ROYAL BOTANIC GARDENS   GRAMPIANS RAINFOREST TOUR

SYDNEY

TOUCH A KANGAROO

PHILLIP ISLAND (PENGUINS!)

FITZROY ♡

HALLOWEEN PARTY!!

Johannes

Maybe it was unkind to feel comforted by the emptiness in your apartment, to treat your heartbreak like a thing I could crawl inside of; but I did anyway and it kept us both warm at night.

Now I can say there are people I've slept with just because we hurt the same way.

Coming Home

It took me too long
to realize it was

not

romantic(, tender, or healthy)

to love someone else
more than I loved

myself.

A Resolution

I swear every poem I write for you is the last one.
I swear this is the last one.

Baggage

I said I'd never write another poem about you,
but everything is a metaphor for the way that we left each other.
Birds flying south for the winter. Rivers running to the sea.
The moon stuck struggling in its orbit
and never really going anywhere
at all.

The other day a coworker asked me how you've been
and I thought that he was joking. It took me
a full minute to put it together.

I've gotten so good
about not flinching at the sound of your name
that people don't know I'd still throw myself
mouth-open into the ocean
for the chance to drown somewhere you might see it.

A Clean Break

I wear rubber gloves around my house
for fear of contracting germs
or coming into contact
with some part of this place
that still has your fingerprints on it.

When I find your lip print stuck to a coffee mug
tucked away in the back of my cupboard,
I pull the mug out and leave it
on the kitchen counter
just to stare at the absurdity of it.

I think *maybe I don't have to get rid of it.*
I think *maybe I'll take care of it later.*
I think *maybe I'll just leave it there for good
and wear the gloves a little longer,*

get some more disinfectant,

*wash my own mouth out with soap
for almost saying your name.*

Just Like You

The first time I deleted your number
from my phone,

it felt like my veins were full of
syrup. Everything felt heavy,
but everything was

sweet
sweet
sweet.

The Second Apology

I'm sorry for trying to love you
before I knew what I was doing,

before I knew how to be wanted
in the light by another person,
before I knew how to look in the mirror
and see something worth holding onto,
before I knew that wanting you
had a name
and that it was okay to say it.

This is no longer an apology to you.
It's one to myself

for the times you said kissing me was
just friendly,
for the months I fucked boys
and thought about your mouth,
for the nights in your bed and the days
on the other side of the room,
for the years I thought it was romantic
to be a secret,
for the size of that closet.

YOU ARE GOOD AND YOU
ARE WHOLE AND YOU
ARE NOT ~~ALONE~~ ALONE
OR UNWANTED OR WEAK
OR STANDING AT THE
EDGE OF SOMETHING ~~WILD~~
THAT YOU CAN'T COME
ALL THE WAY BACK FROM.

The Ocean Always Looked Like You: Reprise

At the beach,
I put my ear to a conch shell
and tell myself
I only hear your name.

It sounds an awful lot
like just the ocean.

Ask Your Mother About Starving

You were born hungry, baby.
You were born with an open mouth and empty hands.
You came into this life with a starving heart.
I know better than anyone that you cannot fill it
with fence posts or china patterns.
All those replaceable things
they say add up to a good life.

You can't fill it with people either.
Don't go trying to build your home like a house of cards
in the mouth of a lover who breathes too hard at night.
They're only going to knock you down.

You are almost always going to want more
than someone else can give.

Almost always.

Barefoot Molly

Once, we made plans to start a band and call it Barefoot Molly. Once, we bought a temporary tattoo from a twenty-five cent machine and I fake-tattooed your ass in the bathroom of Regal Cinema. Once, we sat in your mother's minivan parked on the road in front of my house and you held my hand while you asked why nobody else wanted to kiss you. Once, you spent six months sending me nudes and then pretended it never happened. Once, I said I'd do anything for you and I meant it. Once, you told me you'd never loved anyone the way you loved me. Once, we slept curled around each other on your parents' fold out couch and you woke me with a mug of hot tea in the morning and it felt like life was moving too slow. Once, you called yourself the Sam to my Frodo. Once, you called my heart a bitter animal stuck in a trap. Once, you Skyped me just to sit in lingerie and play love songs on your old guitar. Once, you made me take photos of you laying on my bed in lingerie for your new boyfriend. Once, when you were making dinner, you asked me not to watch you put together your secret pasta sauce but I did from the hall, and it was mostly just Campbell's Tomato Soup and crushed garlic. Once, you chased me through that kitchen with a video camera and we were both laughing and laughing and laughing.

This Went All Wrong

You were never supposed to be a choice.
You were never supposed to be a lesson,
a hurdle,
a thing to learn from
and overcome.

So That's About It

The voicemail you left
on my twenty-second
birthday is still stuck
in my phone. And by
stuck, I mean I can't
bring myself to delete it.
And by *in my phone*, I
mean I got a new phone
so I actually transferred
it to my laptop.

Sometimes I listen to it
when I can't remember
what you sound like.

Thames St.

When I woke today,
my whole front lawn was dotted with dandelions.
All I could think about
was that summer we spent in Baltimore
when her hair turned out yellow in every photograph we took,

and how I haven't been back since I kissed her
with a mouth full of gelato
and she laughed against my teeth.

I never tell the whole truth in my poems.
I wanted them to be better than us.

The Muse Bites Back, Or The Poem In Which
I Berate Myself Because She Won't

after Yena Sharma Purmasir

I KNOW THEY SAY
THERE ARE TWO SIDES TO EVERY STORY,
BUT I DON'T THINK I'VE READ
A SINGLE TRUE THING
YOU'VE WRITTEN ABOUT ME.

I DON'T KNOW
HOW YOU COULD MAKE A LOVE STORY
OUT OF WHATEVER THAT WAS,
HOW YOU COULD TURN ME INTO THE VILLAIN
WHEN YOU'RE THE ONE WHO LEFT.
REMEMBER: YOU'RE THE ONE WHO LEFT.
YOU'RE THE ONE WHO ASKED
FOR YOUR BOOKS BACK
AND BOUGHT A PLANE TICKET
AND NEVER SPOKE TO ME AGAIN.

I CAN'T BELIEVE YOU WROTE ALL OF THAT DOWN.
I CAN'T BELIEVE YOU QUOTED MY LOVE LETTERS.
I CAN'T BELIEVE YOU USED MY VOICEMAILS.
I CAN'T BELIEVE YOU TOOK THIS PRIVATE THING
AND USED IT TO GET YOUR FOOT IN THE DOOR.

Okay

I couldn't sleep last night because I don't know
what you eat for breakfast anymore. I don't know
if you still wear my old clothes or if you threw them out
when you threw me out.

I read somewhere that it's okay to miss people
even if you don't want them in your life anymore;
and I hope that's true. I hope everything I feel is okay.

I just want to leave your name on a page somewhere and never need to come back to it.

A Love Poem For Myself Because I'm Sick Of Writing About You

I hope one day
somebody loves you
so much

that they see violets
in the bags under your eyes,
sunsets in the downward arch
of your lips

that they recognize you
as something green,
something fresh and still growing
even if sometimes
you are growing sideways

that they do not waste their time
trying to fix you

So You're Engaged — So What?

I found out secondhand
and skipped
all five stages of grief.

(I went right to tequila.)

Ongoing Construction

When I think of our separate futures,
I picture concrete chipping away,
and the ghost of our happiness
dancing on top of the rubble.

Reminder For Times Like This:

Embrace the days
on which you are still hurting.
Sore muscles have always
been a sign of growth.

The Blue Lagoon

Autumn. Cheeks flushed from the cool air. I wore my grandfather's flannel shirt over my dress instead of a coat. You pulled off your gloves in the driver's seat. Held a warm palm to my cheek. Asked me what kind of face to make to get someone to want to kiss you. Instead of flirting, I started quoting *The Little Mermaid*. I ran inside afterwards, straight up to my room. Sat on the edge of my bed with two fingers pressed to my lips. Singing "Kiss The Girl" in your car was the first time I'd ever wanted to put my mouth on your skin.

The night you told me that the more people I kissed, the dirtier I would become, was the first time I wondered why anyone would ever want to put their mouth on your skin.

I guess neither one of us came away clean.

Unsent Text Message

I dreamt about you
three different times
last night.

I need this to be over.

38 Days

I am still cutting my hair over the bathroom sink and taking the weather personally. It's been a year since the last poem. Since the last time I picked up a pen and thought about writing your name somewhere on the page. Everything feels so small in your absence. My whole world could fit on the head of a pin.

Body Language

Conversations about her always start the same way. Someone asks: *what does your tattoo mean*?

And I say, *I loved somebody too much once.*

They shake their head like I don't know what I'm talking about, like I'm one of those parents with selective hearing. They shake their head and point. *No, not that one. The one on your foot.*

I say, *every part of me means the same thing.*

Leftovers Pt. 2

I do not believe all love has an expiration date;
I just believe ours did.

I have put to shame every night I thought I wouldn't
get through without you.

Thank You

The smell of your hair puts my stomach in knots.
I want to lay roses at your feet.
I want to pray at the church of your hands.
I want to thank you for every awful thing you ever did to me.
No one will ever be able to knock the wind out of me again.
Not like that.

Not like you.

37 Days (Reclaiming The Bee)

Still writing about you feels like needless repetition.
It feels like sneaking into a neighbor's backyard
just to look around.
It feels like carving my own name
into anything I can get my hands on.

Still writing about you feels like screaming
into someone else's abyss.
A void that echoes back and back and back:

I AM NOT YOURS.

YOU ARE NOT MINE.

I WILL NEVER MAKE THIS MISTAKE AGAIN.
YOU CAN LOVE AND LOVE AND LOVE
AND YOU STILL WON'T BELONG TO ANYONE
AND NO ONE WILL BELONG TO YOU.

IN THE END WE WON'T EVEN HAVE THE PAIN OF IT.

YOU WERE NOT THE FIRST THING TO STING ME
AND YOU WILL NOT BE THE LAST.

I STILL HAVE
A LOT OF GROWING TO DO
AND I KNOW THERE IS
MORE ROOM FOR IT
IN YOUR ABSENCE.

It's All So Light

Nobody is in love with me and everything is still warm. Still soft.
Still rosewater and a typewriter ribbon. Still cookbooks and salt
air and sheer black lingerie. Still red lipstick. Still mostly kind.
Still often uncomplicated. Still mints at the bottom of my purse,
hair held back, pulse thumping through skin. Still sweet tea in
a pitcher on the kitchen counter, a cold glass with three lemon
slices, a full ice cube tray.

Ode To The Purple Mug I Found In Marshalls

God, it will feel so good
to have something warm
to wrap my hands around
at two in the morning
again.

Think of the quiet days
we'll spend together.

Think of the packing and unpacking,
the leases, the emptiness of moving,
the homes we'll leave behind together.

The tableware you won't match with.
God, think about that.
Think about how out of place you'll look
next to my great grandmother's china teacups
and all the silverware I've pilfered
from work.

I'm living alone
and I still don't have my own dishes.
Last month, I lived entirely
off of paper plates.

Say you'll come home with me
anyway.

Loud, Loud, Loud

In a dream,
I see you walking out of the post office
and I swallow my pride like a lit match.

I say,
I'm sorry for hurting so publicly.
I know I didn't have to make so much noise.

29 Days

The morning you marry your true love, I will have an ex-boyfriend laughing somewhere because I told him that it was foolish to be jealous of you; but it was always you. It was you before I moved in with him and it was you after I left. It is not still you, but sometimes I do wake up with a pit in my stomach that goes by your name.

The morning you marry your true love, I will ball my hands into fists and sink like a worm into the bottom of a bottle of fine silver tequila.

The morning you marry your true love, at least three people will say to me: *I thought you'd let this go already.* I will try to explain that leaving you is something I am still trying to process. I will try to explain that letting go comes in waves. I will try to explain that even when we didn't appreciate each other anymore, you still felt like my other half. Sometimes you still feel like my other half.

The morning you marry your true love, everything will taste like quiet panic. Like being startled by house-sounds in the dark. Like walking up to the wrong person in public. I will keep trying to picture your hand with someone else's ring on it.

The morning you marry your true love, I will block out the memory of you sitting across from me in a café on Main Street, whispering like you were worried he could hear you from three states away.

The morning you marry your true love, I will have a mouth full of regret. I will be stuck six feet deep in the memory of your fiancé calling me up just to gloat, to say that he had won. Like you were a thing to be won. Like there was ever any competition. I will recall laughing, saying, *you can have her*. Hanging up the phone. The sound of it is ugly. It does not feel like me. It does not sound like me.

Maybe it will be more than a mouthful.

The Perseids

it's late and i am thinking
of the voicemails i never left you.
all that time i never spent pleading
with your machine.

the fight i did not put up.

the difference it would and would not
have made.

the last time i saw a meteor shower
i thought about the taste of your shampoo
and how your hair might look
pooled on my pillowcases again.
even after
we hated the sound of each other's voices
i still wouldn't have minded
pulling your hair
from the shower drain,
but you don't know that.

i like to think i'm over it.

i like to think one day i will have stories
that don't all start with your name.

i like to tell myself that i wasn't
really in love with you but even on the months
i forget to pay my credit card bills,
i still remember to check your horoscope.

A List Of Things That Remind Me Of You

turtleneck sweaters / violin cases / eating chocolate icing from the jar / 7am / writing letters / checking the mailbox / checking the mailbox again / black ankle boots / minivans / bad parking jobs / gelato / custom lingerie / fake red roses / post-it notes / mix CDs / obscure indie music / 9:30 Club / that one E.E. Cummings poem / holding hands at the movies / Birdies Coffee Shop / cornfields / honey spice rooibos tea / polka dots / pianos / pool tables / hot chocolate / cinnamon / the way it feels when you ache and ache and ache and then sink to the bottom of the bathtub and for just a few minutes it doesn't ache anymore

The first time I really heard my own name, it was in your mouth.

I Still Forget We're Not Even Friends

I still wake up
with things to
tell you.

One day, I won't.

I will learn placid acceptance.
I will stop panicking when I can't perfectly remember
the pitch of your voice
or the curve of your jawline.

The smell of cinnamon won't
make me sad anymore.

At this point it's not about finding someone
to replace you. I have spread my love
all over the place.

It's about trying to sleep
knowing

I live in a world that
has your hands
in it.

This Is What The Poems Are For:

telling other people the things
I can no longer tell you

24 Days

I found one of your old perfumes
in that suitcase you lent me
when I moved off of Uhler Lane.
Instead of throwing it away,
I unscrewed the cap
and emptied what was left of the bottle
onto my bedroom floor,
spent the next few days
unable to sleep
without a window open.
I'm still airing you out of that room.

Lemon And Honey

For my sixteenth birthday, my mother threw me a Sour Sixteen instead of a sweet one. We sent out green and yellow cards. We ate large slices of lemon cake. You and I weren't friends yet, but you were someone else's date in every one of those photos.

For a short amount of time, you lived next to a beekeeper. You gifted me honey in a repurposed jam jar and I left it in the cupboard until it crystallized. I thought that this meant it was ruined.

There are other truths but these are the ones that stick with us even now.

Chameleon

I am different more often than I am the same.
I don't know how anybody falls in love with me.
I don't know how anybody keeps up.

19 Days

I read somewhere
that love only gets old
    if you let it.

I can't remember why we stopped
writing love   letters
and started crying drunkenly into the phone.

I can't remember when we stopped
watering our roots.

I can't remember when we started
competing for the sun.

I tell everyone
who asks about you

        that we outgrew each other.

I still don't know if that's the truth.
Maybe we just got

    tired.

The Third Apology

I don't want to talk about the things that we said.

I want to thank you for spending years fighting with me even when we weren't on the same side. I want to thank you for all of your loud opinions and the maple gingersnap gelato and most of the letters. I want to thank you for making me feel like I was never alone, for battling distance and almost always coming up okay, for seeing me through the worst days. The depression when neither of us knew what to call it. The bad friends. The poor choices. I want to thank you for the poems and the songs and the comics. All of that endless creating we did together. All of that laughter. The hand-holding. The showing up. I want to thank you for always showing up.

You used to tell me that I only had to stay strong until you came home. I just try to stay strong all the time now.

I hope you do the same.

IT WOULD BE A SHAME
TO LOOK BACK ON THIS
AND (OUT OF BITTERNESS)
NOT CALL IT LOVE.

Forgiveness

For the nights that bled into crusty-eyed mornings. For the
boys with vodka breath taking up too much of the bed. For the
bruises and everything that has ever pinned me down. For the
misunderstandings and the overfull stomachs and the messed up
lipstick. For the times I missed the train. For the bad roommates
and the busted AC and every time I got my period in brand new
underwear. For the times I wanted to die and every pen that ran
out of ink and all of the house plants I've killed out of neglect.
For catcalling. For the pets that went to live on farms but really
didn't go to live on farms. For throwing up from drinking and
throwing up from jellyfish stings and throwing up from crying.
For the years I thought I had to be pretty and quiet. For the news,
every day. For western black rhinos going extinct. For broken cell
phone chargers. For bad weather on good hair days. For saying
yes when I really meant no. For sitting alone at the bar on my
twenty-second birthday. For missing the flight. For anxiety and
fruit going rotten and spilling nail polish all over the kitchen
floor. For wanting to kiss someone and never saying anything
about it. For the people who don't like my poems and the times I
have been followed home from the bar and every argument I've
had with my mother about my sexuality. For lost luggage and
people who don't have the heart to change. For toothaches and
heartaches. For finding out that neither of us could bear to stay.

15 Days

I still do not think
anyone could swim in the
wake of you right now.

A Letter To My First Love

Look, I'm not sorry you weren't the first person I kissed. Everybody needs a little practice to get it right. I still don't think I was ever ready for you.

I'm not sorry you weren't the first person I kissed, but I wish I'd met you on the playground. I wish we'd held hands when we were too small for people to make a big deal out of hand holding. I wish I could have kissed you under the slide, pressed you down in the mulch, surrounded by the sounds of hand games and hopscotch.

Look, I'm not saying I'm still in love with you or anything. Things can be important even though they're not important in the same way anymore. You still occupy space inside of me somewhere.

I'm not still in love with you or anything but sometimes when I hear a certain song or drive past my high school, I feel like I'm sixteen years old in a homecoming dress, and we're laughing about boys over our watered down punch. I feel your head slipping down onto my exposed shoulder and I still don't want to move.

Look, I want you to know this doesn't change anything.

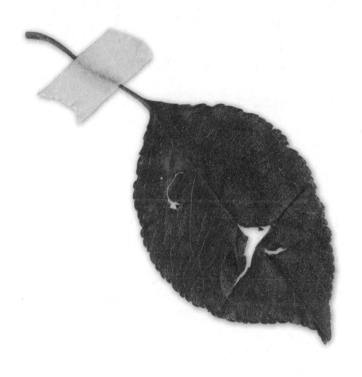

A Series Of Preemptive Wedding Toasts

I WANT TO BE ANGRIER THAN I AM

I STILL DON'T FORGIVE YOUR PARENTS FOR
RAISING YOU TO BELIEVE YOU HAD TO MARRY THE
FIRST MAN WHO TOUCHED MORE THAN YOUR
HEART, BUT I HOPE YOU'RE HAPPY

I FEEL HOLLOWED OUT WITH GUILT TODAY

I THOUGHT ABOUT SHOWING UP AT THAT
CHURCH BUT I DON'T WANT TO RUN AWAY WITH
YOU, I JUST WANT TO KNOW IF YOU'RE OKAY

IN LIEU OF SOMETHING FROM YOUR REGISTRY, I
PROMISED I'D STOP WRITING ABOUT YOU

LOVE IS PATIENT, LOVE IS KIND, I AM NEITHER
OF THOSE THINGS, AND I AM ALSO NOT IN LOVE
WITH YOU ANYMORE

THEY SAY YOU'RE SUPPOSED TO MARRY YOUR
BEST FRIEND AND MAYBE THAT EXPLAINS WHY I
USED TO PICTURE US IN WEDDING DRESSES BUT
IT DOESN'T EXPLAIN HOW YOU WENT THROUGH
WITH THIS

WHAT I MEAN TO SAY IS: I RESPECT YOUR CHOICES BUT I DON'T THINK I'M EVER GOING TO UNDERSTAND THEM

WHAT I MEAN TO SAY IS: I SHOULD HAVE PICKED UP YOUR DRUNK PHONE CALLS BUT I WAS TRYING TO TAKE CARE OF MYSELF

I KNOW IT WOULDN'T HAVE CHANGED ANYTHING

THESE ARE OUR LIVES NOW AND ALL WE CAN DO IS LIVE THEM AS BEST WE CAN AND I HOPE THAT'S WHAT YOU'RE DOING

I HOPE YOU STILL CALL HOME WHENEVER YOU NEED TO AND I HOPE YOU NEVER FEEL STUCK OR HELPLESS OR UNWANTED OR ALONE

I HOPE YOU NEVER THINK ABOUT ME

HERE'S TO YOU AND THE REST OF YOUR LIFE

I WANT YOU TO HAVE EVERYTHING, ABSOLUTELY EVERYTHING

REDACTED VOICEMAIL TRANSCRIPT

I'M SORRY IT'S LATE ▬▬▬▬▬▬
▬▬▬▬▬▬▬▬▬▬▬▬ I'M AT
SARAH'S BACHELORETTE PARTY
AND I'M THINKING OF YOU ▬▬▬▬
▬▬▬▬▬▬▬▬▬▬▬▬▬▬▬
▬▬▬▬▬▬▬ I MISS YOU ▬▬▬
I MISS YOU SO MUCH ▬▬▬▬
▬▬▬▬▬▬▬▬▬▬▬▬▬▬
WE'RE IN A KARAOKE BAR AND I
SANG TAYLOR SWIFT BECAUSE I KNOW
YOU LOVE TAYLOR AND I LOVE YOU
▬▬▬▬▬▬▬▬▬▬▬▬▬▬▬
I'M SO AFRAID OF LOSING YOU ▬▬▬
I'M SO SCARED OF WHATEVER THIS IS

11 Days (Instead Of Calling You)

A poet told me that if I give this up, I will give anything up. If I give this to you, I will have given you everything. I keep thinking that I'm staying away for you but maybe she's right. Maybe it's for me too. Maybe I still want something to hold onto.

I guess that's selfish, which I am told love isn't.
I guess that's why we aren't in it anymore.

My phone lights up in the dark and I get out of bed to look at the stars. I keep your name curled up at the base of my tongue just in case I ever have to use it. I hope that it's you, but it never is. It's an email from the bank, a Twitter notification. I am plagued by late night Snapchats from people who have never heard me talk about you before.

You are getting married in eleven days and sometimes when I want to text you about it, I write about it instead. You are either sick of reading about yourself by now or you don't pay attention to my poems anymore. I don't know which is worse. Sometimes instead of picking up the phone, I pick up the last letter you wrote to me. The one where you lay everything out eloquently:

YOU have a heart like an animal in a snare.
YOU are going to die alone.
YOU are empty.
YOU, YOU, YOU.

Me, me, me. Someone told me once that it helps to remember why we stopped talking in the first place. They weren't wrong.

My phone lights up in the dark and I get out of bed to look at the stars. I take a walk. I think a lot about the moon. About how if I am small then you-and-I are smaller still. A blip somewhere on some cosmic radar. Something that has already happened. Something that is somewhere finished and tucked away. If we both look at the same moon and you still don't want to call to say goodnight then maybe we're not looking at the same moon anymore. Maybe the moon has nothing to do with it. Maybe you're not the same person. Maybe I'm not.

My phone lights up in the day and there is no moon to contemplate. How easy it would be to make a misdial that rang in your kitchen. Instead I grab a coffee with another girl. I put my phone away. I pour myself like sugar into everything she has to say. I don't try to make metaphors out of anything.

Sometimes when my fingers itch for the phone, I pick it up. I call a friend instead and talk to them like a sponsor. I say, *I'm thinking about using again.* They say, *baby, you don't want to go down that road.* I say, *I know, I know, I know.*

I take out your contact information and put it back in again.

Catch And Release

I'm not sure if I believe in poetry as healing
so much as I believe in poetry as fishing lures
baiting you out of me.

On Writing My First Book Of Poetry

When I decided to tell the world how badly I'd loved her,

they called it brave.

As if it were some noble thing I'd done, making a catastrophe out of a mess, setting up a tourist section in my own bed and selling souvenirs.

All of those poems about wanting. All of those poems about her and honey and me throwing myself through the wringer.

It was not brave to break like that. It was not brave to write those poems. It was not even brave to stop.

It was just hard.

The B Word

I kiss the pretty boy in black semi-sheer thigh highs, plant my hands on his hips, pull teasingly at his garter belt and I can hear my mother shaking her head across town. I can't tell if she is disappointed or confused.

I lie awake next to the girl who smells like sweat and lemonade. I think about shoving my face into her hair but she falls asleep talking about her boyfriend. On the day my mother corners me in the kitchen to ask if I'm *A FUCKING LESBIAN,* I say no. I wonder if it counts as a lie when I still don't have a word for all the different kinds of porn I like to watch.

When I come out, I am eight thousand miles away from home. I am sharing the bed of a substitute teacher. He likes to tie me up at night and kiss me in the morning. My mother says she's not surprised but she doesn't understand. When I use the B word, all I can think about is the first time bisexuality came up with her in conversation and she laughed.

THEY'RE JUST GREEDY. IT'S LIKE THEY DON'T EVEN CARE WHO THEY'RE FUCKING. THEY'D FUCK ANYTHING. THEY MAY AS WELL FUCK A DOG.

My grandmother asks where they went wrong, if it's because my father left and you know, the other stuff. She wants to be able to call my sexuality a result of trauma but I won't let her. She says, *LOOK: IF YOU FALL IN LOVE, I'LL BE HAPPY FOR*

*YOU BUT YOU CAN'T MARRY A WOMAN BECAUSE IT
PERSONALLY OFFENDS ME.* She calls me a dyke and says it's
a joke. She never asks me again if I'm seeing anybody.

I have a crush on a femme who makes their living writing good
lines. I swoon every time they call me baby, but I tell them I don't
know if I want to get into things. I second-guess myself into a
corner. What if it is just a phase? What if I change my mind?
Do I really need to put my family through that kind of thing?
I never tell my mother we've been dating but I tell her when we
break up and she still cries for three whole days.

I make arrangements to meet up with a man I'm in love with
and I don't tell anyone in my family because I don't feel like
explaining that it doesn't mean I'm straight. I go to London
alone. When I return, I make up stories about landmarks and
tourist attractions. I tell no one where I really spent my time.

My coworker asks me, *Why do lesbians use dildos? Why don't they
just fuck men?* And I want to say, *have you ever met a man??* but
I feel like the joke is too gay and I'm always trying to convince
everyone I know that my sexuality is a revolving door which
never stops spinning long enough to check IDs.

Still, somehow, I am always getting carded.

OKAY BUT HOW MANY WOMEN HAVE YOU BEEN
WITH? HOW MANY THREESOMES HAVE YOU HAD?
I MEAN ALL GIRLS ARE A LITTLE GAY. YOU DON'T
HAVE TO FLAUNT IT LIKE THAT. YOU JUST DO THIS
TO GET GUYS, DON'T YOU?

When the Supreme Court ruling comes through for marriage
equality, I sob quietly in the bathroom, but I don't know if I
can really celebrate the way that I want to because I don't feel
gay enough to talk about the struggle, but I'm not straight. My
mother finds me in the morning to ask if I've heard the news.
She says, *I SUPPORT YOU BECAUSE YOU'RE MY*
DAUGHTER BUT I DON'T AGREE WITH IT AND I
DON'T THINK IT'S RIGHT.

I say, *then you don't really support me*, and she doesn't say
anything.

LOVE WITHOUT FORGIVENESS
IS NOT LOVE. LOVE THAT IS
UNKIND IS NOT LOVE. LOVE
THAT DOES NOT MAKE YOU FEEL
GOOD IS <u>DEFINITELY</u> NOT LOVE.
LOVE THAT DOES NOT GROW
ANYMORE IS NOT LOVE ANYMORE.

4 Days (Hair Of The Dog)

I was told once
to lick salt before I started drinking
because it would ease the pain the next morning.
Maybe I should have done all my crying before we met.
Maybe if I'd done this out of order, it would feel
different, somehow better.
Or just less.
I was told once
to find part of the animal that ripped you up.
Track down the thing that ran out on you.
Grab whatever kicked your ass last night
and kiss it on the mouth.
I was told once
that the only way through this is caffeine.
I was told once
that the only way through this is exercise.
I was told once
that you just have to shoulder it
and get on with your day
but this morning I got stuck on the way to the shower.
Doubled over on the bathroom floor.
Everything wanted to come up.
The smell of your shampoo.
Waking up next to you.
Your love letters.
The bridge of your nose.
Your red coat.
Everything wanted to come up
but the vodka.
So I let it.
I was told once that's what you're supposed to do.
Throw everything up. Throw everything out.
Go back to bed.
Sleep until it's over.

Roots

There were nights we were so soft,
I could feel her growing next to me;
but just because you grow together
doesn't mean you're meant to stay.
People don't have roots for a reason.
The best thing about intertwining
hands together is that you can stop
when you need to.

I STILL REMEMBER YOU
AS A LITTLE GIRL
WHO OVERWATERS PLANTS
BECAUSE SHE DOESN'T KNOW
WHEN TO STOP GIVING.

1 Day (Gravitational Pull)

Do you think moons really love
the planets they circle around —
like in that poem we used to read
to each other?

I've been thinking: maybe they're
just stuck. Maybe they don't
know how to let go either. Maybe
gravitational pull is just code for
*I don't know how to be away from
you* — but on a massive scale.

Like, *baby, I know we don't work
together. I just forget how to be a
moon when you're not around.*

I forget how to be a moon when
you're not around, but I'm getting
the hang of it. I'm working it out.

My strength is defined, not by what I continue to carry, but by what I have allowed myself to put down.

Dirty Laundry

The first night I slept in your bed,
I got my period, ruined the sheets.
It was the universe stumbling in drunk
and slurring, *this girl, oh–*
this girl is gonna make you bleed.

0 Days

so this is it / this is the big shebang / my whole damn universe / falling headfirst into a black hole / this is the end of my love letters to nostalgia / my love letters to things that don't exist anymore.

honey,
      we don't exist anymore.
      can't you hear the sound of silence out there somewhere?

-365 Days
(On The Occasion Of Your First Wedding Anniversary)

You are always waiting for him
to come home and I am always
writing poems I'm not supposed
to be writing. The ones about my
mother and the ones about your
hair. I'm not sad about this
anymore.

Not in the way everyone thinks.

I almost never sulk about your
mouth. I did today, for a second.
I thought about you pulling leftover
wedding cake from the freezer,
licking thawed icing off your fingers.
You're not my biggest heartbreak
anymore.

What a delicate relief to both of us.

The Baker's Epilogue

A timer counts down in my kitchen and the waiting comes easily. Something about the inevitability feels comfortable and final. When it goes off, I peek into the oven to see if the pie has browned evenly. It needs to sit another minute and there's no use forcing it before it's ready.

Earlier today I went shopping for the apples alone. I used an adapted version of your mother's recipe. I crimped the edges just like you showed me. I've realized that it's not as important to remember where I've learned things, as it is to just learn them. I don't always have to trace everything back to its source.

When the minute has passed, I pull something fresh and full of cinnamon out of the oven. Everything is perfect. Everything is sugar-coated. I don't see you in any of this.

You may have been part of the healing but you don't get to be a part of what's healed.

About The Author

Trista Mateer is a poet from outside of Baltimore, who could be living anywhere by the time you read this. Known for her eponymous blog, she is also the author of four full length collections of poetry, and won the Goodreads Choice Award in 2015 with *The Dogs I Have Kissed*. She is currently working as a freelance editor but still manages to spend most of her time Googling cheap airfare and writing poetry about things that don't matter anymore.

@tristamateer
tristamateer.com

Other Work By Trista Mateer

Instead of Writing Our Breakup Poem

Before the First Kiss

[redacted]

Small Ghost

The Dogs I Have Kissed

[Dis]Connected: Stories and Poems of
Connection and Otherwise

Additional Notes & Credits

The poem referenced on page 135 is "Photograph" by Andrea Gibson.

The title on page 7 refers to Micah 4:4. "Everyone shall sit under their own vine and fig tree and no one shall make them afraid."

Some of these poems can be found in their original format on the internet and in the previous edition of this book. They're not incorrect versions. They're just young.

"The B Word" has previously appeared on *Thought Catalog* and *Medium*.

"A Brief Note on Biphobia" is just that: a brief note. This book is about my personal experience with love and sex and all the tricky labels that go along with those things. It is not intended to be a faultless resource. Below are some actual resources if you have more questions:

> biresource.org
> bisexual.org
> thetrevorproject.com
> cdc.gov/lgbthealth/youth-resources

Acknowledgments

Thank you to Caitlyn Siehl, Ari Eastman, Fortesa Latifi, Amanda Lovelace, and Iain S. Thomas for being part of my poetry family. Thank you to Yena Sharma Purmasir for the advice. Thank you to Charlotte Crawford for loving me. Thank you to Rachel Drummond for the Tim Tams and the tea and the hours spent spilling my heart over the kitchen table in Melbourne. Thank you to everyone who helped me pick up my pieces after she left, after I left, after I came back and kept leaving. Thank you to everyone who is still helping me pick up those pieces.

Thank you to Olivia Jackson, Lydia Havens, Caitlin Clifton, Caitlin Conlon, Danielle Wall, Tiffany Matzas, and anyone else I begged to read and re-read the many drafts of this second edition.

Thank you to Michelle Halket & Central Avenue Publishing for giving this book a home.

And thank you: for your support, for picking up this book, for kissing and crying and holding on too long. Thank you for understanding. Thank you for reading, always.

IF YOU'RE STILL WAITING FOR
CLOSURE, GIVE IT TO YOURSELF.
WHAT DO YOU STILL NEED TO SAY
TO THEM?

AND WHAT DO YOU NEED TO HEAR FROM THEM?

I KEEP A LIST FOR DAYS MY HEART HURTS AND I CALL IT **OTHER PEOPLE FEEL THIS TOO**. IT'S FULL OF MUSIC AND ART AND POEMS THAT REMIND ME I'M NOT THE ONLY PERSON WHO'S GONE THROUGH WHATEVER I'M GOING THROUGH. WHAT WOULD BE ON YOUR LIST?